Real Woman, Fake Woman

(Useful Insights for SINGLES and MARRIED)

Titi Olukoya

Published & Designed by

TREASURE PROJECTS

Printing with a difference

P O Box 8384 Wuse, Zone 3, Abuja
+234 703 472 4872

Printed By: Spotless
+234 906 130 1049

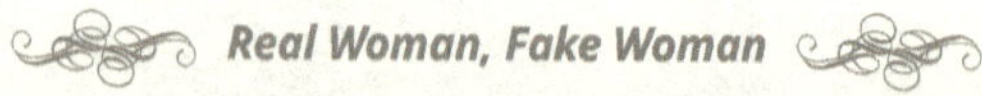

DEDICATION

To my Husband, My Hero, my Mentor, my Earth, my King, my Sunshine, my Love, my life, my everything, who taught me to believe in myself and to be a woman by example. Darling, not only did you mentor me and gave me a reason for living, you made me see the gift in me which had been ignored for so long. I am happy to be part of you.

To the many wonderful women that God has made me to lead. They are epitome of beauty, with the grace and glory of God radiating over their lives. Thank you for making leading and serving worthwhile for me. You are the best and I love you all.

Above all, all glory and honour and adoration be to GOD without whom I would not be alive today.

ACKNOWLEDGMENT

I acknowledge the Jesus Embassy family; pastors, ministers, missionaries, Head of departments, workers, office staffs, ministry partners, friends and families for making service worthwhile.

I appreciate my beloved husband for his impartation, encouragement and mentoring in putting this messages into this book.

I appreciate my children for providing the enabling environment to make serving God interesting.

Thank you so much for your unwavering love, prayers and support.

I celebrate your greatness.

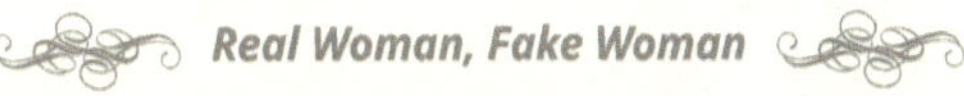

CONTENTS

INTRODUCTION

Every one of us needs inspiration in order to do exploit. God inspires through His word in the Bible, and the insights He gives His servants to impart others. This book is inspired by God to impart the women out there, spurring her to take needed steps in order for her to be what He has purposed that she should be in Him. That purpose is of distinction, of dominion, of standing out, of being different in her generation. That is the daughter God has created, the woman he has conceived as His a reflection of His image. For every daughter of Zion, the Holy Spirit who is in charge in her life is the difference. He makes the difference. But, how many of us give room for Him to ensure we are what God has in His original plan for us? Why is this important? God is ever looking for seven women of honest report, full of the Holy Spirit and wisdom that He may appoint over His business as recorded in *Acts chapter 7.*

Why is this also important? It is important because when God appoints anyone over His business it is an opportunity to do wonders in the life of His appointee. For instance, God turns Deborah into a national prophetess, a respected woman far and near, one that generations after her still remember. This was one woman who would have lived and died as an obscure housewife. God appointed her over His business, she accepted and did it with a difference, and she brought her out of obscurity forever. What kind of woman are you, and what kind of woman do you want to be? How can you be the woman God has in mind, not just any woman? This is dealt with in this book. Here, the point that must not be missed is that when a woman sets herself aside for God, chooses to be different, she has earned a signed but blank divine bank cheque that she can never finish cashing for herself and the generation after her.

This book itself is important at this time because we are in an age in which most women, single or married, do not strive to distinguish themselves in issues that matter to God. They conform to the world, do what the crowd does, and are consequently lost in the crowd. Don't be lost in the crowd. It amounts to lose of a glorious destiny. It is an invitation to living and dying in obscurity. Meanwhile, there is a place of uniqueness that God has set aside for His daughters. This book throws the challenge that we should take it by standing with Him, not with the world. May the Lord bless your heart and spirit as you read in the name of Jesus.

Chapter One

Real Woman, Fake Woman

od's idea of the woman he creates is different from the woman the world expects to see. What God creates is real; what the world creates is a copy, a fake copy meant to meet some other standard that the world has set. Note that God's standard is different from that of the world. Whatever standard the world sets is never the original thing. The woman that conforms to it is fake, just as anything that is contrary to God's idea is fake. Such a woman cannot please God.

She cannot make the kind of difference God wants. This is because the world had created an image of the woman that is contrary to that of God. The woman that walks almost naked in the name of fashion is okay by the world. They even set up communities where only the people who choose to walk naked live.

They set up exclusive clubs for men to exchange their wives with other men. The woman that divorces and remarries eight times is okay by the world. The woman that shows no respect to her husband in the name of equality is okay by the world. That is the world.

The troubling thing is that many women in church buy into some of these evil trends. They key into the way of the world without realizing the error. We are in an age when many women live fake lifestyle.

They take what is the shadow to be the essence of Christianity. They have taken their Christian-sounding names to be what makes them Christians. But Johanna or Hannah does not give a fully description of anyone's personality as a Christian. People bear Christian names but they do what Christ would not do. It's because they are not born again. Many are in church but the church is not in them.

Others see Christianity as their heritage, an identity. They engage in war of words with unbelievers that they have a Christian heritage that they are proud of, yet they are full of sin. It is among them we find higher rate of unmarried young people who fornicate, married women who commit adultery. Those in the other religion see this and they consider themselves even more righteous than those who say Christianity is their heritage. That is the reality around us.

For many, Christianity has become a mere physical tag, a means of physical identification, not a spiritual one. But is this what God has in mind? Note: the fact that a person marries in church does not make her a real woman that God wants her to be. If she is not born again her fruits will show it.

The bible says *"By their fruits you shall know them."* Being the real woman God has in mind is not by saying so, it is not by the looks, not by the name, and not by appearance. It is not even by the Christian family background. Rather it is by the fruit on she displays that she is known that she either belongs to God or not.

What is God's idea of a woman?

She is that woman who remains the epitome of His original creation in soul, spirit and body? She is born again, and she lives it. When we refer to a real woman, we mean one who lives her life the way God has conceived her to live it. She is not interested in living for

the world to praise her. She does not lust after the things of the world and their deception. She is not interested in conforming. She wants to conform to God's plan for her only. She pants after God. She is keen to walk in God's will. She wants to retain the same image that God has for her.

She is a woman who is not only born again, but she is broken, thirsts for the Lord and married to Him. She is sold out to God, her heart and eyes are focused upon Him. This is a continuous process. Conforming to God's image of a woman continues for as long as we live. We work it out day after day. No one arrives there in one day. But with Him in us we can do all things.

REAL WOMEN IN THE BIBLE

There are examples of women in the Bible that we can follow as we make this effort. Sarah is one. There is Deborah, Ruth, the slave girl to Naaman the war general, Esther, as well as the virtuous woman in *Proverbs 31.*

The life of each of these female persons points our attention to different issues that any daughter of Zion needs to be conscious of. Sarah, for instance, is an example of the kind of wife God expects his daughter to be. The truth is that anything short of the kind of place Sarah has in the life of her husband is contrary to what God has in mind for a wife.

The quarrelsome, nagging wife is not God's idea. The wife who is ready to file divorce papers at the slightest marital disagreement is not God's idea of a wife. The unfaithful, Godless wife is never his idea. None of this was found in Sarah. One cannot imagine God paying a divine visit (as he did to Abraham and Sarah) to the home where wife goes one way and the husband goes another way. That is confusion.

God is not the author of confusion and he does not dwell in confusion.

What Sarah showed for us to emulate is wisdom for a married woman in how to run her home. There will always be marital issues. Sarah and Abraham had theirs. But Sarah did not walk away. It is wisdom for a married woman to be determined that no matter what happens, she would make her marriage work.

She must see her marriage as a project. It is wisdom for her to determine that her project would not fail, that she would fight for her marriage. If there is nothing else she can do, she can pray and whatever is faulty with the marriage God will repair.

There are fine details or controversies in any marriage that make people to warn to pack it up. But here, it is important to leave them and concentrate on the need for a woman to take charge of a wobbling marriage though prayer.

In any case, it is the fact that she does not take charge in the place of prayer that the marriage is wobbling in the first place. Any approach apart from prayer may end in frustration and wreck the marriage. But through prayer, nothing shall be impossible.

Sarah is an example of how a wife could get her husband to be her best friend. She showed Abraham honour, she showed him respect. This is the basic expectation of any husband and he is more than likely to respond to it with love and care. God's mindset is that the wife shows her husband respect as the head of the family. It is wisdom that she conforms to God's original idea.

In doing so she would enjoy peace and happiness. Rebecca is an example of a maiden and a wife. She showed kindness to a stranger and found her man. Many ladies have lost this virtue.

Between man and woman, God has imbued woman with a heart of kindness, generosity, hospitality, gentleness or meekness. The woman is created strong, yet gentle. She is of a gentler spirit, kinder, more patients compared to man.

God does not make mistakes. A woman has to be like this. The role God has fashioned her to perform requires it. For through her children come into the world and she has to raise them. Patience is needed to raise children successfully.

Rebecca displays those virtues God has deposited in a woman. They are ever there, hiding somewhere, until a woman decides to bring them out. A woman may consider herself impatient or aggressive. That is a lie of the devil. It is because she allows herself to manifest such traits. If she prays for it, God can restore the original spirit of patience, gentleness and meekness that he has created in her as a woman. Sometimes, this is what it takes to win back a husband who is behaving strangely, refusing to pay his wife attention as he used to.

Deborah was a prophetess in Israel and a wife. This tells a few things. She was married, but she did not neglect the gift of God in her life. She developed it, walked in it, yet she was married. Many daughters of Zion have gifts of God that the world awaits to see and benefit from. But they do not use them. They sit and relax, losing sight of the need to develop themselves in the area of their gifts. This is not God's plan. It cannot be, and this is why he gives us Deborah as an example in the Bible. Here is what the Bible says concerning her in

Judges 4:4 & 8-9 (KJV);

"And Deborah, a prophetess, the wife of Lapidoth, she judged Israel at that time...And Barak said unto her, If thou wilt go with me, then I will go: but if thou wilt not go with me, then I will not go. And she said, I will surely

go with thee: notwithstanding the journey that thou takest shall not be for thine honour; for the Lord shall sell Sisera into the hand of a woman. And Deborah arose, and went with Barak to Kedesh."

Ruth demonstrates the extent to which honour shown to husband's family especially his parents, can take the wife. The Bible gives us a view of her life in **Ruth 3:11;**

And now, my daughter, fear not; I will do to thee all that thou requirest: for all the city of my people doth know that thou art a virtuous woman.

How God places Ruth in a lineage (that of Jesus) that makes us remember her till today is closely linked to how she shows honour and kindness to Naomi, her husband's mother. As a rule, God rewards a person who honours elders.

Many women these days do not want to have anything to do with their in-laws. True, some in-laws may be problematic. But the real woman takes charge of issues concerning them through prayer, asking God for grace and his intervention, rather than adopting a combative approach. No woman can dishonour her in-laws and hope she is doing the right thing.

No daughter of Zion should take that route. For it can impact a marriage, and of course, the law of sowing and reaping should be remembered. Ruth showed honour and kindness to her mother-in-law and God specially positioned her to remain evergreen.

The slave girl to Naaman the general of the Syrian army was not living in Israel. She was in Syria in the household of her captors as noted in **2 Kings 2**

Kings 5:1-4 (KJV);

Real Woman, Fake Woman

One could picture a girl that serves the wife of this general to be between fourteen and twenty five years old. The wisdom with which she passed information to her master indicated that much.

One thing that was clear was that she did not forget the God of her parents even though she was far away from home. She had been well brought up in the way of the Lord in Israel, and wherever she found herself she did not depart from it. Her mother must have ensured she knew the God of Israel.

The girl therefore ended up witnessing to her master to go after the living God for solution to his leprosy. One can assume that her mistress must have seen her lifestyle that was different from that of other slave girls to take her word for it, and pass the information from the slave girl to her husband.

Naaman's wife must also have trusted the girl's loyalty, honesty and trustworthiness. Not many girls exhibit these traits these days. The fault can be traced to mothers.

The real woman is a good example to her children through her devotion to God. Esther is an example of a real woman in many ways.

She shows how a daughter of Zion should live her life as an unmarried girl and a wife.

There is something that must serve as restraint, something that makes an unmarried girl refrain from defiling herself. Without such a restraint she will misbehave freely.

The most potent is her fear and love for God. When a girl loves God and fears him, she would keep herself. She will wherever she finds herself. This is missing these days. But it was what kept Esther, making her God's candidate for the throne. As aspect of her life is caught for us in ***Esther 2:15-17 (KJV);***

> *"Now when the turn of Esther, the daughter of Abihail the uncle of Mordecai, who had taken her for his daughter, was come to go in unto the king, she required nothing but what Hegai the king's chamberlain, the keeper of the women, appointed. And Esther obtained favour in the sight of all them that looked upon her. So Esther was taken unto king Ahasuerus into his house royal in the tenth month, which is the month Tebeth, in the seventh year of his reign. And the king loved Esther above all the women, and she obtained grace and favour in his sight more than all the virgins; so that he set the royal crown upon her head, and made her queen instead of Vashti."*

Unlike Esther, these days many go to the altar to wed with pregnancy. It is the way of the world. It does not see it as anything bad, and many women in church have accepted this and even advise younger ones to get pregnant first before they go to the altar. They forget that immoral lifestyle is a destiny destroyer for any woman.

It has consequences that sometimes we are not even aware of. It limits, and digs pit that many later discover they have fallen into in their life's journey. The real woman keeps herself because she loves God and wants to honour him with her body.

The virtuous woman is well-spoken of in **Proverbs 31:10-20 & 27-29 (KJV);**

"Who can find a virtuous woman? for her price is far above rubies. The heart of her husband doth safely trust in her, so that he shall have no need of spoil. She will do him good and not evil all the days of her life. She seeketh wool, and flax, and worketh willingly with her hands. She is like the merchants' ships; she bringeth her food from afar. She riseth also while it is yet night, and giveth meat to her household, and a portion to her maidens. She considereth a field, and buyeth it: with the fruit of her hands she planteth a vineyard. She girdeth her loins with strength, and strengtheneth her arms. She perceiveth that her merchandise is good: her candle goeth not out by night. She layeth her hands to the spindle*, and her hands hold the distaff. She stretcheth out her hand to the poor; yea, she reacheth forth her hands to the needy….She looketh well to the ways of her* household, and eateth not the bread of idleness. Her children arise up, and call her blessed; her husband also , and he praiseth her. [29] Many daughters have done virtuously, but thou excellest them all."

Why must any woman pay attention to the virtues noted in **Proverbs 31**?

They are God's expectations of her daughter and anything outside of this indicates that something is not what it should be. In all, there are enough examples one can cite in the Bible if one desires to conform with God's idea regarding a woman. For God has the original plan of what he wants the woman, married or single, to be. It is the real plan. Whoever walks according to that real plan is the real woman.

FAKE WOMAN

Just as we have good examples so are there bad ones in the Bible. Sapphira must come up for mention as a woman who conducted herself contrary to God's idea. She was a fake woman, a fake Christian. It is important to note this because here is a wife that agrees with her husband who embarks on deceit. When husband and wife agree to follow a path that is not Godly it is a clear indication they are both not born again.

Many who say they are Christians are like this. Wives agree with their husbands to do what they should not as seen in the example recorded in *Acts 5:1-8;*

> *"But a certain man named Ananias, with Sapphira his wife, sold a possession, And kept back part of the price, his wife also being privy to it , and brought a certain part, and laid it at the apostles' feet. But Peter said, Ananias, why hath Satan filled thine heart to lie to the Holy Ghost, and to keep back part of the price of the land? Whiles it remained, was it not thine own? And after it was sold, was it not in thine own power? why hast thou conceived this thing in thine heart? thou hast not lied unto men, but unto God. And Ananias hearing these words fell down, and gave up the ghost: and great fear came on all them that heard these things. And the young men arose, wound him up, and carried him out, and buried him. And it was about the space of three hours after, when his wife, not knowing what was done, came in. And Peter answered unto her, Tell me whether ye sold the land for so much? And she said, Yea, for so much."*

Many wives in the church are privy to evil. They are aware of the evil that their husbands engage in and they fail to take a stance against it. She too is not born again, just like her husband. Birds of a feather flock together. Someone once said there was a man as well as his wife who were known to be pastors but they engaged in acts of bribery and corruption where both of them work. My response had been that bearing the title of pastor is one thing, being born again is another.

Anyone can bear any title. There are many people who are not born again but they bear Christian-sounding titles. They are living

  *Real Woman, Fake Woman* 

examples of Sapphira and her husband. My observation is that much of the time, husband and wife tend to be of the same mindset. If the husband is rude, the wife tends to be the same. If one is combative, belittles people and keeps malice, the other is more than likely to be of the same disposition. They even discuss their quarrelsome and rude exploits at home and agree they are right.

When one is not born again, the other is not likely to be born. It is the reason they meet each other, like in each other, and agree to marry in the first place. Note that it does not matter that both attend church or bear Christian names. It does not mean anything that they are even ordained ministers in the church. Genuine salvation takes what is not right away from the person concerned. When people retain in their lives what Jesus says he does not want, their salvation is suspect. For those small foxes constitute barriers at the gate of heaven where Jesus says he will tell even those who perform miracles in his name that he does know them because of their evil acts.

A real woman of God, born again, would never agree when her husband is walking in error. There are many women in the church who are like Saphira. It is the reason most are not making a difference. There is also the example of Jezebel who had a man killed because she wanted his vineyard for her husband. How she sets her husband, Ahab, up for evil is recorded in ***1 Kings 21:5-7 (KJV)***;

> *"But Jezebel his wife came to him, and said unto him, Why is thy spirit so sad, that thou eatest no bread? And he said unto her, Because I spake unto Naboth the Jezreelite, and said unto him, Give me thy vineyard for money; or else, if it please thee, I will give thee another vineyard for it: and he answered, I will not give thee my vineyard. And Jezebel his wife said unto him, Dost thou now govern the kingdom of Israel? arise, and eat bread, and let thine heart be merry: I will give thee the vineyard of Naboth the Jezreelite."*

Jezebel also wanted to have the head of Prophet Elijah cut down because he was against her action and that of her husband. She did not achieve the latter because God rescued his servant.

12   But this same spirit of murder lives on. Like Jezebel, Herod's wife in the New Testament had the head of John the Baptist who spoke against her action brought to her on a platter. She passed this same spirit to her daughter who was able to carry John's decapitated head and was not afraid. Many in church have the same murderous spirit. They murder others with their tongues. They cut people down to nothing. They nurse bitterness against others in the church. They are unforgiving. They focus on the fault of others, and see nothing wrong in destroying people's reputation.
No born again person can be like this. May God deliver us from the spirit of Jezebel.

These women were bad influence on their husbands, their family and the society. They were greedy about material things. They had wrong attitude to life. They had power but used it wrongly.

Chapter Two

laying
The Foundation

o one can conform to God's idea regarding any matter until her foundation is properly laid. Foundation has to be laid before any woman can hope to conform to God's idea for her life. Nothing can be built on nothing. No house is without a foundation.

A Christ-like lifestyle must have its foundation in Christ. It starts from the circumcision of the heart performed by Christ himself. Without it, one is simply a Christian by name, a church attendee, nothing more.

Anything done outside a proper foundation in Christ amounts to self-help, walking in the flesh, and the person is not likely to make headway. It is the reason we see many of the ungodly issues that are found among so-called believers.

For the so called Christian whose foundation is not properly laid, being a church member is like being a member of just any other worldly association. She does not see any difference in both. How then can she conform to God's idea in anything? Such a person cannot assimilate the fact that God's kingdom operates by a different set of rules. She cannot comprehend it that the church is the body of Christ in whom nothing impure must be found. She cannot, because she does not have an encounter with the One who can open her spiritual eyes and heart through the Spirit. Her spiritual foundation has not been touched and relayed.

For the person in church who has not been so touched, it is like expecting an unclean water pot to pour out clean drinkable water. If the reader could consider the kind of encounter Paul the persecutor of the church had which turned him into the greatest among God's evangelists, then she had an idea of the point being made.

That many who say they are Christians do not have such encounters is one reason the church has challenges with the attitude and action of most of its members. Many do not know the difference between the church and any other association formed in the world, and it shows in their lifestyle. Some of such actions are unprintable, alarming to put it mildly.

One of our fathers in the Lord said each time cases about members of the church were brought to his attention his heart would take a dive. He said he would ask himself: Can this be happening in the church?

It had also been said that the General Overseer of The Redeemed Christian Church of God, Pastor E. A. Adeboye, said he had stopped asking the Lord to show him the spiritual files of people, church members. It must be because what he saw in the lives of many was unprintable.

When the foundation is missing in the life of a church member, this is what happens. It is a real challenge. If anyone wants to be a real woman and make a difference in her generation the foundation of her relationship with God is the number one issue to settle. The following is a check list:

BE BORN AGAIN AND GROW IN THE LORD

The primary foundation for any Christian is to be born again. What does it take to be born again? It takes hearing the word of God, realize that one has fallen short, repent and confess one's sins to the Lord, confess Jesus as one's Lord and Saviour, as well as invite him into one's life. From that moment one begins to walk according to the will of God. Also, everyday one takes the steps needed to grow in the Lord. How is this done?

Renew the mind

Growing in the Lord is a continuous process. One of the needed steps is to renew one's mind. This is to be done on a daily basis as advised in ***Romans 12:1-2 (KJV);***

> *"I beseech you therefore, brethren, by the mercies of God, that ye present your bodies a living sacrifice, holy, acceptable unto God, which is your reasonable service. And be not conformed to this world: but be ye transformed by the renewing of your mind, that ye may prove what is that good, and acceptable, and perfect, will of God."*

Renewing the mind is like changing the water in a baby's feeding bottle each day. It is like pouring out boiled water in a vacuum flask and refilling it with fresh boiled water. As a mother, the reason this is done is obvious.

Renewing the mind is like having a stream that comes from a clean source and which flows without ceasing. The water in this stream is cleaner than the water in a stagnant pond. When water is stagnant it will be polluted and becomes bad for drinking.

The mind of a born-again Christian must be constantly renewed. If this does not happen it will start to accommodate little foxes that eat away at one's righteous standing with God. It is a real danger into which many in church have fallen. When a so-called Christian starts to justify things that are contrary to what the word of God says, it is the sign of a mind that is not constantly renewed. The greater danger lies in putting into action those things that are contrary to the word of God which one justifies. Such can make one lose salvation without even realizing it.

HOW TO RENEW THE MIND
-Read, study and meditate on the word of God
-Pray Always
-Praise God Constantly
-Thank God in all things

Be filled with the Holy Spirit and power

To walk with God, one needs the Holy Spirit. Many work and serve God in the flesh. They have yet to receive the baptism of the Holy Spirit. It is burdensome to serve God without the baptism of the Holy Spirit.

Jesus knew his disciples would not be able to handle the task he gave them effectively after he must have left the earth without the help of the Holy Spirit. This was why he said they should wait until he sent the Holy Spirit to them. The apostles waited and they received the Holy Spirit as recorded in *Acts 2:1-3;*

Acts.2.1 - And when the day of Pentecost was fully come, they were all with one accord in one place.
Acts.2.2 - And suddenly there came a sound from heaven as of a rushing mighty wind, and it filled all the house where they were sitting.
Acts.2.3 - And there appeared unto them cloven tongues like as of fire, and it sat upon each of them.

The Bible further tells of the importance of the Holy Spirit in the life of a Christian in *Romans 8:14-15 (KJV);*
"For as many as are led by the Spirit of God, they are the sons of God. For ye have not received the spirit of bondage again to fear; but ye have received the Spirit of adoption, whereby we cry, Abba, Father."

The Holy Spirit helps a born-again Christian in so many ways. He gives strength when one is weak physically. He gives direction on what to do. He keeps one's heart at peace in times of storm. He gives boldness to speak God's word without fear. He can put words in one's mouth that resolve disputes that have become problematic. The Holy Spirit can help one to overlook offence.

One reason many find it difficult to forgive offence is because they are not baptized in the Holy Ghost so they cannot give the Holy Spirit a chance to minister to their heart when they are hurt. As a result, they engage in self-help – rivalry, writing petition etc. – meanwhile, self help can lead to more errors.

In addition, it is by the Holy Spirit that one prays and instant healing happens. It is by the Holy Spirit that one commands and it happens accordingly. A Christian who has yet to be baptized in the Holy Ghost may struggle with a lot of issues, including sin. One needs to seek the baptism of the Holy Ghost. It is a fundamental foundation of living in conformity to God's idea regarding anything.

How To Receive The Holy Ghost
>*-Avoid sin.*
>*-Constantly ask God for the baptism.*

Give God devotion

Devotion to God must be the centre of the life of any Christian. It is a foundation for any other thing one wants to do or achieve. When God has our devotion he takes care of other issues concerning us.
The Bible has this to say in ***Luke 24:10;***

> *It was Mary Magdalene, and Joanna, and Mary the mother of James, and other women that were with them, which told these things unto the apostles.*

Devotion is not just about the prayer time. It is about total commitment, trust, reliance on God. When a woman is devoted to God, she does not have any other power, counsellor or solution that she depends on to resolve issues that concern her. She totally focuses on God to make a way where there is no way.

Devotion is about serving God with all of one's heart. It is about working for God in the church, taking care of the pastors and their families, and the body of Christ. When one's heart is sold out to God, she has no time for gossip, backbiting, jealousy, busybody, stealing church's money and property, engaging in covetousness. Those who are devoted to God spend their time looking into his word, praying, preaching his word on the street and in their neighbourhood, and imparting God's word in their children.

Be a worshiper

A life of worship summarizes what God means to a believer. It tells of the extent of her faith in the God she professes. No matter what happens, she worships God. When a woman is of this disposition she has what is required to impart others and what she does. Without this foundation in her own life, she may be a bad influence, advising others to take steps that make them sin against God.

A real woman must be a real worshipper of God as is noted in ***Galatians 4:27 (KJV);***

Gal. 4.27 - For it is written, Rejoice, thou barren that bearest not; break forth and cry, thou that travailest not: for the desolate hath many more children than she which hath an husband.

When Sarah offered her dried body to God a son broke forth! Moses offered a rod, the staff with which he had led sheep and a serpent broke forth. Be a worshipper all day, all week long.

On **Monday**, *tell God, "You are the Lord, that is your name..."*
On **Tuesday**, *sing to him, "Jehovah reigns..."*

On **Wednesday,** *tell him, "I just wanna be where you are, dwelling daily…"*
On **Thursday,** *"… I will praise you, oh my Saviour…"*
On **Friday,** *say, "…aka marama kam ga akoro - chineke moo…"*
On **Saturday,** *sing, "…let everything that has breath…"*
On **Sunday,** *say, "…there is something that makes me come…"*

The Bible says, let everything that has breath praise The Lord. The only qualification to praise God is breath. If there is life there is hope. The believer who worships God hands over all her battles to him. Real women do not fight their battles by themselves. They do not go about insulting and engaging in physical assaults. They do not nag their husbands, rather they go to God in worship and prayers. They allow the Lord to fight for them as it is stated in ***Exodus 14-14;***

Exod. 14.14 - The LORD shall fight for you, and ye shall hold your peace.

Have the right attitude

The right attitude is about making up one's mind to honour God in every way possible, no matter what happens. It is about choosing to humble oneself before God and do what pleases him only under every circumstance. It is about deciding to be on God's side even when everyone else is going the way of the world.

Right attitude is about deciding that God is always right, and one will do what pleases God no matter what the risk is. Right attitude has to do with honouring servants of God and fellow believers, to be at peace with them. All of these are crucial foundations to making a difference.

When a so-called Christian chooses to do what pleases herself only, it is the outset of disobedience. It is a wrong attitude, and she will be doing the exact opposite of what God desires from his children. What positive difference can such a person then make to her generation?

Chapter Three

Being Different, Making A Difference

What is in a person is what she can manifest. No one can give what she does not have. The last section makes a prescription regarding what must be within, the foundation that must be laid in a believer that must be different and make a difference. Once that is settled, it is time to manifest, to affect the world around us.

Jesus says without him we can do nothing. To do exploit is not by physical strength or force of arm. Excelling in anything does not depend on the hard work or the physicality. Rather it is by the grace that God releases upon a person. Every good gift and every perfect gift comes from God.

A person may do so little physically but God enlarges and magnifies that little by his spirit. A person may be in one place, but God makes her to affect lives all over the world. It is by grace. It is by the spirit of God. It takes grace to stand apart, to make a difference. In order to key into such grace, the believer who desires to be different and make a difference must observe the following:

Be sold to God

A believer that must be different, and who wishes to make a difference must be sold to God spirit, soul and body. Her mindset is to do God's will. At a time most people go the way of the world she does not. Her heart and soul are for God. She lives her life to please God. The Bible has a comment on this in **1 Corinthians 6:19;**

1Cor.6.19 - What? know ye not that your body is the temple of the Holy Ghost which is in you, which ye have of God, and ye are not your own?

The believer who wants to be different cannot be like Lot's wife. Lot's wife went the way of the world. She was more interested in the things of the world. She looked back and she missed it.

One of David's wives went the way of the world, mocking the man in her life for being so devoted to God and she missed it. Jezebel went the way of the world by imbibing murderous witchcraft spirit and hence she missed it. God's idea is that her daughters are different like Esther. They deny themselves like Ruth. They are sold to God like Deborah.

Be Obedient

God's idea is that his daughters obey him completely. How can God be our father if all we do and say are contrary to his expectation? A legitimate daughter takes pleasure in obeying her father. She knows her father would love her for it and reward her.

God demands obedience from his children. Obedience is the primary basis of our relationship with God. If it is missing we cannot claim God as our father. It is also a requirement if one must get the best from God as the Bible states in **Isaiah 1:18-20 (KJV);**

"Come now, and let us reason together, saith the Lord: though your sins be as scarlet, they shall be as white as snow; though they be red like crimson, they shall be as wool. If ye be willing and obedient, ye shall eat the good of the land: But if ye refuse and rebel, ye shall be devoured with the sword: for the mouth of the Lord hath spoken it."

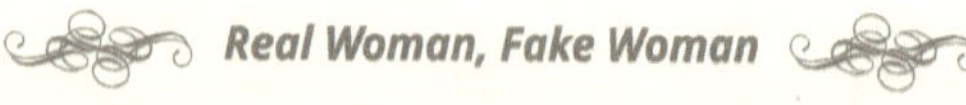

There are instructions in the Bible as to how the single lady should live. Obey them. There are instructions regarding relationship with the spouse. Obey them. There are instructions about how to raise children in the way of the Lord. They are to be obeyed. In obedience there is blessing of the Lord. There is grace to do exploits, stand apart.

Let the Holy Spirit lead

Many misbehave so much because they do not submit themselves to be led by the Holy Spirit. They do not make themselves teachable by the Holy Spirit. They do not acknowledge the role of the Spirit of God in the affairs of a believer. They ignore the Holy Spirit, so they engage in self help rather than God's help. The outcome is that they take on battles they should not. They go into businesses they should not. They marry persons they should not have married. They laise with people that can be the sources for their downfall. They walk into traps set by evil-minded people. They quarrel with others when they should have kept their peace.

Note that God did not save us only to abandon us to self-help. He saves us so that he can take charge, carry our burdens and resolve our issues. He does this through the Holy Spirit who dwells in every believer, and the Bibles says this in **Galatians 5:22;**

Gal.5.22 - But the fruit of the Spirit is love, joy, peace, longsuffering, gentleness, goodness, faith,

God is looking for a woman who will who will make the Holy Spirit her teacher, her companion, her lover. A woman led by the Holy Spirit will not fall into errors, and she will overcome all her challenges.

However, when a believer lets her flesh and her mind rule her, she is missing out on something fundamental in the heavenly race i.e. the help and leading of the Holy Spirit. Why did Jesus promise his disciples the Holy Spirit when he was about to complete his earthly mission? He knew the Holy Spirit would help, guide, lead, teach, and comfort the believer. It was because he knew the believer would be committing too many errors if she engages in self-help.

Jesus knew without the help of the Holy Spirit the believer would be rising and falling. He knew the world could make a believer miserable if the Holy Spirit were not available to comfort her. It is by the help of the Holy Spirit that the daughter of Zion can live a commendable lifestyle.

When he leads he helps his daughter to be a worthy example, not a bad example. That way she is able to make a difference wherever she is.

Embrace Wisdom

Wisdom is a spirit. The Bible says Jesus is the wisdom and power of God. It is the Spirit of God who imparts wisdom. When he dwells in any believer, her ways will be different. She will see things, do things, and say things differently. It is not by herself. It is the Spirit that dwells in her.

The Spirit makes her excellent in what she does. Concerning the place of wisdom in the life of a believer, the Bible has this to say in *Proverbs 9:9*;

Prov.9.9 - Give instruction to a wise man, and he will be yet wiser: teach a just man, and he will increase in learning.

God's idea of a woman who is different and would make a difference is one who embraces wisdom. Wisdom is the principal thing. God is looking for a woman full of wisdom.

A wise woman builds her home. She does not do things

anyhow. She does not act in anger. Rather she allows the Holy Spirit to minister to her on what to do and say. She does all things guided by wisdom. It takes wisdom for a woman to effectively rule her world, her home, her family, her finances, and enjoy favour from her spouse. Wisdom in speech, character, attitude, behaviour, and in relationship with the opposite sex is essential, otherwise a person might find herself embroiled in issues that are best avoided. Refusal to embrace wisdom is the reason many in church find themselves in situations that should not mentioned among believers.

Have honest report

As Christians, we are God's saleswomen, his representatives, his image on earth. He expects that we represent him well. Therefore, what people say about us with regard to honesty, trustworthiness, and integrity is important.

Many in church cannot be trusted with anything. This is not a Christ-like lifestyle. It is important to have a honest report because that is the Bible that people around believers read. People who do not know Christ watch Christians to see if there is anything different about them. Honest report is one of the things they look out for. What should an unbeliever make of a church attendee who tells lies, fornicates and lacks personal integrity?

Of course, the unbeliever considers herself more righteous and sees no reason why she should take the church attendee seriously. God is looking for a woman who is honest, not a woman that will collude with her husband to tell lies like Saphira. He wants us to possess a good testimony before men and women. People should be able to testify of us at the gate of our enemy that indeed we are believers.

Be filled with love

God is love. His Holy Spirit fills a believer's heart with love. The believer that is filled with love is filled with God. How come the attitude of many women who are supposed to be believers shows hatred for others? It is because the spirit of love has yet to permeate and sit in their heart, spirit and soul.

There is a way the spirit of love dwells in a person such that she loves even those that hate her. It needs to be experienced to be believed. People can abuse a believer yet with the help of the Holy Spirit she would feel like giving them a hug. This is what love can do if one allows him to have a place.

It is true that people may hurt one's feelings. But when the Spirit of love dwells in one's heart and one permits him to minister he frees one's spirit to the point one wants to laugh and hug those who cause offence. God is looking for individuals who will give his Spirit of love a chance to minister and help them when people around are proving difficult. It is such individuals that can make a difference wherever they are, not people who respond to hate with hate. Respond to hate with love and you will stand out as God has purposed.

The Bible talks extensively about love in *1 Cor 13: 1-end.* God is looking for a woman who will break her alabasta box, a woman who will love God for who he is, who will forget herself and love him unconditionally through obedience to his commandment regarding love.

Showing love no matter what happens has its benefits for the believer. Joy will fill her heart. She radiates joy all the time. It is because she chooses not to carry burdens. She chooses to free herself from the yoke of unforgiving spirit. Nothing can hold down her prayers, her progress, her blessings. She cannot be trapped by the devil. She is

God's idea of the woman that can make a difference in her generation.

Love must be the basis for anything a Christian does. It was the basis for the work of salvation that God did for mankind. For God so loved the world. Actually, actions that are love-based announce a person beyond her immediate environment more than anything else. It brings recognition. It spreads fame. Mother Theresa who worked with destitutes in India all her life was known all over the world. She was given some of the highest awards. When she died, Heads of State knelt down beside her casket in appreciation of the love she showed the world.

Another person is Bill Gates. This man founded Microsoft Computers. At one point, he had around 60 billion US dollars as personal wealth. Then he decided he would not leave that kind of money to his children. He invested 33 billion in helping the poor, combating malaria across the world.

Soon, Heads of States and Government began to associate with him for this worthy cause. When he requests to see Queens, Presidents and Prime Ministers, doors are open to him. Act of love lift. It announces. It promotes. It is a foremost measure of making the most difference in one's small corner.

Be a giver

Giving is the surest path to receiving blessing. One can give in different ways. One can give of oneself through service to God and to others. One can give using money or other material things.
Giving could be about setting time aside to preach the gospel to unbelievers. Giving has its spiritual implications. It is a means of storing treasures in heaven. The returns are bountiful.
The Bible talks about giving in *Psalm 126:5;*

Ps. 126.5 - They that sow in tears shall reap in joy.

Tabitha was a giver and as a result she got her life back, as recorded in
Acts 9:36-38;

Acts.9.36 - Now there was at Joppa a certain disciple named Tabitha, which by interpretation is called Dorcas: this woman was full of good works and almsdeeds which she did.

Acts.9.37 - And it came to pass in those days, that she was sick, and died: whom when they had washed, they laid her in an upper chamber.

Acts.9.38 - And forasmuch as Lydda was nigh to Joppa, and the disciples had heard that Peter was there, they sent unto him two men, desiring him that he would not delay to come to them.

The Shunamite woman was a giver and she got the blessing that she lacked in the process. When a believer expects something from God, giving is an opportunity for God to remember and act. Break something for God through giving just as that woman in the Bible broke her Alabasta box.

What precious things can we break for God? It is when we do that he concludes we are ready to be empowered to make a difference in our generation.

Imbibe an attitude of thanksgiving

One needs to have the right attitude towards thanksgiving. It is a factor if one must make a difference. In order to have outstanding performance God's help is needed.

To receive God's help in great measures, the attitude to thanksgiving must be right. We have so much to thank God for. In reality, many of the things we do and consider as service to God in and out of church are channels of saying **"Thank you"** to God. How will it then be possible for a person who cannot say **"Thank you, God"** in every way possible to make a difference?

What is thanksgiving?

Thanksgiving is an attitude. It is an orientation that no matter what happens, one must show gratitude to God. Something must be different in the life of the person who thanks God all the time. This is because it is the will of God, and the Bible says so in *1 Thessalonians 5: 18;*

1Thess.5.18 - In every thing give thanks: for this is the will of God in Christ Jesus concerning you.

Thanksgiving is an attitude God wants us to put on, to wear like a garment. This is what is stated in *Romans 1: 21;*

Rom. 1.21 - Because that, when they knew God, they glorified him not as God, neither were thankful; but became vain in their imaginations, and their foolish heart was darkened.

Many of us find it difficult to thank fellow human beings who do us favours. In fact, many repay good with evil. It is difficult to comprehend how some turn their back against someone that God has used to assist them before.

It is a great evil. A person who makes herself the enemy of people who have helped her is missing out on something. For it is an error that God cannot overlook. It does not matter what the reason is. As believers we should be able to forgive, remember the good deeds of the past and be thankful.

How can a person who makes herself the enemy of someone that God has used to help her make a difference? This is an offence against God. For she is ungrateful. Many in church do the same thing to God.

Take a look at the ten lepers. They cried to Jesus for mercy. These were people that should not approach Jesus at all according to

Jewish law. But they approached him and he healed them. Only one of them returned to offer thanks.

Many get good things from God but they use their tongues to show ingratitude. The Psalmist says bless the Lord at all times, that his praise shall continually be in his mouth. For some, their problem is their tongue. They never see or say anything good about life. They cannot offer thanks for what they have now. Yet the scripture says life and death are in the power of the tongue. A lady gave birth and on seeing the baby the first thing she used her tongue to say was something negative about the baby.

How can God be happy about this? Many breed naughty children, and complain about them. The issue may be their attitude towards thanksgiving. God gives them children but they say ungrateful things about them.

There was this person who waited for seven years and finally his wife gave birth to a baby boy. When he was asked how the first year birthday was going to look like, what came out of his mouth was that everyone should wait to see whether or not the child would clock a year on earth. What an ungrateful father.

The first thing to do is to appreciate God for anything one gets, for what God has done and what one expects God to do. Ascribe greatness to God through thanksgiving because his work is perfect and all that he does is just.

IMPORTANCE OF THANKSGIVING
It turns situation around for the better
Most people enjoy safe business trips, official trips, multiple streams of income, miracles, blessings, healings, unexpected visitations. How many of these do they

remember to thank God for? Instead, they are ever complaining about the part that they expect God to do something about. When a wife has a spouse that causes her pain, it is time for her to check her attitude.

For being married in the first place, has she shown gratitude to God, or does she complain about the husband always? Why is this important? Many want to be married but they are not. Has God been given thanks for that spouse? Is that spouse appreciated or he is treated as though he is just another item of decoration in the house? That may be where the root of the problem is. The spouse is a gift, and until he is appreciated as a gift, it may be difficult to get the best out of him. Change attitude to thanksgiving over that spouse and there will be changes in that home.

It brings about total deliverance

When God gets the thanks he brings about total deliverance. The Bible says something about this in **Luke 10:17-21**;

Luke.10.17 - *And the seventy returned again with joy, saying, Lord, even the devils are subject unto us through thy name.*

Luke.10.18 - *And he said unto them, I beheld Satan as lightning fall from heaven.*

Luke.10.19 - *Behold, I give unto you power to tread on serpents and scorpions, and over all the power of the enemy: and nothing shall by any means hurt you.*

Luke.10.20 - *Notwithstanding in this rejoice not, that the spirits are subject unto you; but rather rejoice, because your names are written in heaven.*

Luke.10.21 - *In that hour Jesus rejoiced in spirit, and said, I thank thee, O Father, Lord of heaven and earth, that thou hast hid these things from the wise and prudent, and hast revealed them unto babes: even so, Father; for so it seemed good in thy sight.*

When the seventy returned they did so with thanksgiving, and they had testimony of total deliverance. They recorded that Satan fell like lightening before them from heaven. Every sickness, every form of attack in the lives of people was destroyed. Every chain and shackle of the enemy was broken. Captives were set free. God added more beauty, glory, and honour to their lives.

It is the secret of success

Thanksgiving is the secret behind great success. Concerning people who are full of thanksgiving others would wonder what their secret is. The Bible says when there is a casting down then shall we say there is a lifting. Thanksgiving is a factor. Whoever keys into thanksgiving and wears it like a garment has taken hold of the key to success.

It is a prayer of faith

Whenever we show thanksgiving, God arises on our behalf. For it shows that we have faith he can do what has yet to be done. This is noted in *John 11:14;*

John. 11.14 - Then said Jesus unto them plainly, Lazarus is dead.

It is an effective weapon of warfare

When the believer engages in thanksgiving, her faith is lifted up, burdens removed, and she is encouraged. Every spirit that makes one to struggle in the place of prayer disappears. Thanksgiving is a reason God fights battles for his children according to *Exodus 14:14;*

Exod. 14.14 - The LORD shall fight for you, and ye shall hold your peace.

When Peter was in prison the church rose on his behalf

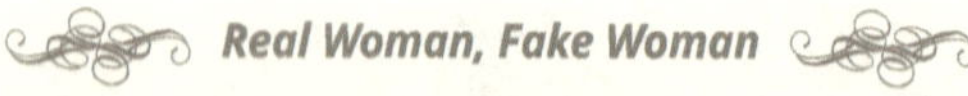

with a prayer of thanksgiving and he was set free. The same happened to Paul and Silas. They sang of God's faithfulness and the angel of the Lord was sent to rescue them. Engage thanksgiving, it is at the root of any victory achieved in the life of a believer.

Thanksgiving is soul winning

Thanksgiving is a means of winning soul. When people see the attitude of a believer towards thanksgiving, when they see how grateful she is for every single thing God does, they are encouraged and their faith is strengthened.

When people see that a believer is not married, they see she has no baby, no good job, no accommodation, no food on the table, yet they see her bubbling for God they are won over. When they see the believer laughing, smiling, rejoicing, serving God and most especially when they hear her positive confession towards life, people are attracted to God. The believer's lifestyle alone can be enough testimony of what God means to those who serve him.

Often it is not when the believer holds a microphone that she preaches to unbelievers, her life of thanksgiving to God can be a sermon. It is evangelization, and the Bibles says whoever wins soul is wise. She becomes a candidate for God's greater grace to do more exploits. The Bible says this in **Psalm 57: 4-11**;

Ps.57.4 - *My soul is among lions: and I lie even among them that are set on fire, even the sons of men, whose teeth are spears and arrows, and their tongue a sharp sword.*
Ps.57.5 - *Be thou exalted, O God, above the heavens; let thy glory be above all the earth.*
Ps.57.6 - *They have prepared a net for my steps; my soul is bowed down: they have digged a pit before me, into the midst whereof they are fallen*

themselves. Selah.

Ps.57.7 - My heart is fixed, O God, my heart is fixed: I will sing and give praise.

Ps.57.8 - Awake up, my glory; awake, psaltery and harp: I myself will awake early.

Ps.57.9 - I will praise thee, O Lord, among the people: I will sing unto thee among the nations.

Ps.57.10 - For thy mercy is great unto the heavens, and thy truth unto the clouds.

Ps.57.11 - Be thou exalted, O God, above the heavens: let thy glory be above all the earth.

As well as in *1 Samuel 22:1-2;*

1Sam.22.1 - David therefore departed thence, and escaped to the cave Adullam: and when his brethren and all his father's house heard it, they went down thither to him.

1Sam.22.2 - And every one that was in distress, and every one that was in debt, and every one that was discontented, gathered themselves unto him; and he became a captain over them: and there were with him about four hundred men.

Helps to avoid pitfalls – Thanksgiving makes heaven see to it that a believer is guided to avoid pitfalls that the enemy has put on her way. One mistake that many believers make with regard to thanksgiving is that they do not ascribe victory, favour, progress, good health to God. In the process, they miss out on the mercy of God to take pits away from their path, or expose it before they get there. The story of Samson shows this in *Judges 15:1-end.*

This greatest problem and the cause of Samson's downfall is not women or his sexual impurity. His mistake was his lack of gratitude. He was not recorded to have ascribed any glory, honour and praise to God in all that he did. He thought all his achievements were by his own power. For each victory in battle, deliverance, or help from God, Samson never took time to say thank you to God. He attributed all the success to himself. Everything was all about 'I' as shown in Verse *3 of Judges 15*.

Judg. 15.3 - And Samson said concerning them, Now shall I be more blameless than the Philistines, though I do them a displeasure.

Yes, a woman knew the secret of Samson and got her captured. But this was avoidable. Heaven would have assisted him to know of the danger ahead. Since he did not factor God into anything anymore, it was easy for him to miss the red light even if heaven had signaled it, just as he had ignored his parents' warning that he was neither meant to take strong nor marry an unbeliever. May God help us to live a life of thanksgiving.

RUN WITH A DIFFERENCE

The believer who wants to make a difference must run her race with a difference. Salvation is a race. Final salvation, to make heaven, is a race. Living in the world is a race. One cannot do things the way the crowd does it and expect to make a difference.

Many run, but the person who outruns others to clinch the prize must have done something that others do not do. That is the way it works. Many women sit and do things like the rest of the crowd. In serving God, in prayer, in giving they are not different from the crowd. But whoever wants to be extraordinary must do the extra. She must be different from the rest.

The Bible points to this in 1 Corinthians 9:24; "Know ye not that they which run in a race run all, But one receiveth the prize? So run that ye may obtain..."

Every person on earth is involved in a race. We need to be mindful how we run. What difference can we make as a child, teenager, worker, or minister is a question we should constantly ask as believers wherever we find ourselves. We must not join the crowd to complain while we do not lift a finger to do something about a challenge. God did not save us to complain. He saves us so that we may make a difference.

In *2 Kings 5:2-3,*

2Kgs.5.2 - And the Syrians had gone out by companies, and had brought away captive out of the land of Israel a little maid; and she waited on Naaman's wife.

2Kgs.5.3 - And she said unto her mistress, Would God my lord were with the prophet that is in Samaria! for he would recover him of his leprosy.

The slave girl in the house of Naaman was a nobody. But she did not focus on her status. She did not give excuses that she had challenges with her status in the society. Instead, she made a suggestion that changed the life of another person. She used the available opportunity to make a difference.

Never focus on challenges. Those who do cannot make a difference. But it takes the grace of God not to focus on challenges. This is why closeness to God in order to tap the needed grace is necessary. Whoever focuses on challenges will not take a step that can change her destiny. She cannot change the destiny of the people she is positioned to affect.

Challenges must not make a believer abandon her responsibilities, leaving so many things undone. The Bible says we run in a race.
It takes one's totality – mental, physical, mindset – to be involved in a race and win. So what choices have we made? Have we chosen to win, stand out, be different, or remain in the crowd? It is all about choice. The decision a believer makes today will determine the level of the difference she makes tomorrow. Be a woman who can add value to life, add spice to marriage, add spice to the people around. When the word of God says in *1 Corinthians 9:24,*

it means the believer is supposed to obtain something. What each believer wants to obtain becomes the question. Whether or not she wants to obtain becomes her choice to make.

For God does not only want the believer to run, he wants her to obtain. What does it mean to obtain? To arrive, to receive, to be appreciated for affecting lives, to be given a prize, to receive an award, to stand out, to be the best, and most especially to receive the crown at the end of the day. Note that every successful person takes her chance at specific stages in life's race. She passes through challenges to become the award winner. The people who win awards and stand out do not just get it.

It takes them constant practice, dedication, endurance, perseverance, and diligence. It is time to say enough of doing things the same way and getting the same result. Why not try another approach, run with a difference and get an outstanding result?

HOW TO RUN WITH A DIFFERENCE

Be Determined

Determination is a state of the mind. Never look back on that dream. It takes determination to make a marriage work, make a business boom, ensure that the children excel.

It takes constantly taking one's condition to God for guidance and resolution. How often we read, study the word, and table our plan before God is important. It takes a determined person to set aside time to do these in this age when there is so much distraction.

David determined not to let lion and bear devour his

father's sheep and God helped him. He could have watched and later give excuses to his father. But he did not.

Those exploits added up to make him stand out and make a difference in his generation. The man who would kill Goliath had already killed lion and bear. Never lose focus no matter what the situation is. Never lose focus of Jesus even when things change for good. Be determined to remain in him and run the race as God desires. The Bible promises that there are rewards in *Exodus 15:26;*

Exod.15.26 - And said, If thou wilt diligently hearken to the voice of the LORD thy God, and wilt do that which is right in his sight, and wilt give ear to his commandments, and keep all his statutes, I will put none of these diseases upon thee, which I have brought upon the Egyptians: for I am the LORD that healeth thee.

Be Industrious

The believer should consider whatever she lays her hands on as a project that must not fail. It cannot be abandoned. This takes industry, resourcefulness. According to *Proverbs 10:4;* Be industrious.

Prov.10.4 - He becometh poor that dealeth with a slack hand: but the hand of the diligent maketh rich.

Enough of abandoned projects. It is important that the believer is faithful in whatever God has deposited in her hands. This is what is said in *Proverbs 21:5;*

Prov.21.5 - The thoughts of the diligent tend only to plenteousness; but of every one that is hasty only to want.

God does not bless the lazy. He blesses the work of the

hand of a hardworking person, not her laziness.

The person that fails as an engineer is not likely to succeed as a pastor. Whoever cannot manage people's cloth as a tailor might not be able to manage people at all. Many believers are industrious when they become born again. But as the years roll by, they relax. The believer cannot relax. She must keep running.

Keep learning at his feet -

Our race is a marathon. The marathoner must take water to refresh. Just as a runner must nurture her body to sustain her strength, the soul must be fed constantly. The Bibles says so in **Proverbs 13:4;**

Prov.13.4 - *The soul of the sluggard desireth, and hath nothing: but the soul of the diligent shall be made fat.*

The soul must be nourished with the word of God. The Psalmist says in **Psalm 119:11;**

Ps.119.11 - *Thy word have I hid in mine heart, that I might not sin against thee.*

as well as in **Psalm 107:20;**

Ps.107.20 - *He sent his word, and healed them, and delivered them from their destructions.*

No matter what the challenge is, it is the word of God that will deliver and set free. The believer must use the word of God to frame her life, that of her children, her husband, her destiny.

Ignore sin

Running the race is easier for the believer who ignores sin. Sin is a load. It is a burden that one does not need in a race.

 *Real Woman, Fake Woman* 

It weighs one down. The person who runs a race but carries load cannot go far. Sin stagnates. It stalls the work of deliverance. It reverses gains made. It blocks opportunities. Sin of disobedience to God is likened to witchcraft.

Any believer that wants progress in life must not dip her hand in sin of adultery, stealing etc. Any woman that wants progress in other aspects of her life must submit to her husband as the word of God admonishes. Have time for the children. Take care of the home. Disobedience to God's command in these areas can slow a woman down.

Enlist in the Lord's army

Be in the service of God. Be a soldier for him. Enlistment makes the race easier to run. Every born again Christian is automatically enlisted in the army of the Lord. Take another step, be a worker in his vineyard. Get busy. Be occupied with the word of God. An idle man's heart is the devil's workshop.

The training in the Lord's army toughens and makes one rugged, ready to withstand the storm when the enemy shall raise it. Note that there is time for the storm of every believer. Many fall on the wayside because they have not prepared themselves.

There are battles in the race. Enlistment in the Lord's army helps to overcome them at each stage. The battle that the believer has to confront is not against flesh and blood. To win, she needs to put on the whole armour of God, according to ***Ephesians 6:11;***

Eph. 6.11 - Put on the whole armour of God, that ye may be able to stand against the wiles of the devil.

God wants us to be courageous and go into the battle. He will supply the strength as noted in *Isaiah 26:4;*

Isa.26.4 - Trust ye in the LORD for ever: for in the LORD JEHOVAH is everlasting strength:

Never compromise faith

It takes faith to do the impossible. The Bible says in *Hebrews 11:38;*

Heb.11.38 - Of whom the world was not worthy:) they wandered in deserts, and in mountains, and in dens and caves of the earth.

every runner believes she can win, and that is why she is in the race in the first place. But many are in church and they do not put their faith in God for healing in their body, finances, wayward children, troubled marriage.

Why are they in church then? They seek for solutions somewhere else. This is compromise. God wants his children to have faith in him for anything. For with him, nothing shall be impossible. As a result of their lack of faith, many find the race difficult to run. It is because they do not see God as the ultimate solution to every issue. The result is that they fret and dabble into things they should not. They compromise their faith. By faith the believer can achieve what people say is impossible.

Get tested through trails

Expect trials. There cannot be victory without battle. Wait for trials and confront them head on as they come. This is the lot of the believer. Do not flinch. God does not expect his children to flee on the day of battle. Know that in this race one's faith will be tested. People will mock. They will discourage. It is part of the trial, but the believer must not turn back. For victory is assured.

COURT WITH A DIFFERENCE

How a believer manages herself as a single lady will affect the
course of the rest of her life.

Many make mistakes at this stage. Sometimes, such mistakes lead to
wrong choice of spouse, or delayed marriage. Courtship is fraught
with dangers. Many miss it here and they miss it big. When one courts
right, she is likely to get it right for the rest of her life. For she gets the
foundation right.

Courtship is a period of casual or close friendship between
two unmarried people of the opposite sex. Courtship is a period when
two people come together to find out through close observation and
interaction if they belong to one another. Courtship comes after
engagement and not the other way round.

These days many things go wrong during courtship. An
interaction with singles would show that many of them are passing
through pains, challenges, hurt, frustration, and abandonment.
Often, the two people in a courtship are not celebrating one another,
or each operates on different frequency.

Whatever the believer is passing through, observing the
following rules may save her heartache and lead to a fulfilling
relationship.

Rules to observe as a single sister

Let God be the foundation of the courtship

For any believer, God must be the initiator and foundation
of every relationship intended to lead to marriage. Note
that whatever God does not ordain, God does not sustain.

Many struggle with their marriage because they disobey this key factor. Even in the church it is not every courtship or marriage that is truly founded on God. That is, many marriages are not entered into with the full assurance that this is God's will for the parties involved.

Many believers still select their spouses the way the world does. They choose spouses for all manner of reasons, many of them unconnected with the will of God.

Having a good job, a good house, a car, fat bank account is still revered among born again Christians. These things are not bad but they are not all that is required in a Christian marriage. What does God say about the suitor is? We know the testimony of a sister who has confirmation that a brother is God's choice for her at a time the brother does not have a job. He has nothing to impress her. But they pray together and God opens doors.

People also mention love. Yes, love is fundamental. Attraction to the other party is equally good. But there is still the need to pray through and be sure it is God's will. We had heard of the story of two believers in love, but when both decided to go for deliverance ministration together the man ran away when the sister began to manifest. That was the end of the love. If he was sure she was God's choice for him, he would not run away. This is why many do not mind calling it quit with their marriage. It is because they do not lay it on the foundation of God's will in the first place.

There are couples in church who say they meet through matchmakers. That is the way of the world, not the Bible.

The matchmakers of this world use physical and emotional things to come to their conclusions. But God checks the spiritual.

That two people are physically and emotionally compatible does mean they are spiritually compatible. God is a spirit. So he is concerned first with the spiritual aspect to any marriage. It is the more important element.

Many people who think they are compatible are actually not spiritually compatible and this is the root of the problem they experience in their marriage. God is the matchmaker, and no matter where a believer meets her spouse, if she does not pray through to know God's will she is walking an unknown path full of risks. Make God the foundation, and he will be there to sustain in the day of storms.

Do not convert in order to marry

There are single sisters in church who say they do not mind marrying unbelievers. The Bible has something to say about this in *2 Cor 6:14-18;*

2Cor. 6.14 - *Be ye not unequally yoked together with unbelievers: for what fellowship hath righteousness with unrighteousness? and what communion hath light with darkness?*

2Cor. 6.15 - *And what concord hath Christ with Belial? or what part hath he that believeth with an infidel?*

2Cor. 6.16 - *And what agreement hath the temple of God with idols? for ye are the temple of the living God; as God hath said, I will dwell in them, and walk in them; and I will be their God, and they shall be my people.*

2Cor. 6.17 - *Wherefore come out from among them, and be ye separate, saith the Lord, and touch not the unclean thing; and I will receive you,*

2Cor. 6.18 - *And will be a Father unto you, and ye shall be my sons and daughters, saith the Lord Almighty.*

Pay attention to this:
What fellowship --- righteousness ---- unrighteousness
What communion --- light ------ darkness
What concord --- Christ ---- Belial
What part --- believer --- unbeliever
What Agreement --- temple of God --- Idols

Choosing to marry an unbeliever in disobedience to God's command is rebellion. Whenever there is a rebellion in the Bible the enterprise ends in confusion. God is not mocked, whatever a believer sows she shall reap. It takes a sister in church who is not born again, convicted and broken to choose to disobey God by marrying an unbeliever. This is the reason youth/singles must be rooted in Christ. When they are spirit of error will not have a root in their lives.

Avoid the carry over effect

Many born again Christians still carry over their past lifestyle, their lust, anger, jealousy, and unforgiving spirit. This is wrong. The Bible says in **2 Cor 5: 17;**

2Cor.5.17 - Therefore if any man be in Christ, he is a new creature: old things are passed away; behold, all things are become new.

God takes over the believer's emotion, character, action, attitude and remould it to conform to Christ. But many do not allow themselves to be remoulded and they carry it into their relationships. Thus, during courtship, the man lusts to the point of forcing the sister to have sex with him.

We know this is sin. But many courtships have fallen victim of lust of the flesh, which becomes a hindrance to running the race smoothly and effectively. As a single sister, every ungodly behaviour must be abandoned for God's way of life. Worldly pleasure must not be carried into the new relationship in Christ.

Avoid Pharisee relationship

Pharisee relationship is a pretentious relationship. People engage in sinful acts while they pretend to others in church that nothing is going on. It is ungodly. Avoid it. Every relationship between a sister and a brother must be in the open. The pastor must know what is going on and prayerfully guide.

Do not be involved in canopy relationship

This means a sister and a brother do not clearly define what is going on between them. Yes, they relate but what they want with each other and where they are going is not clearly defined and agreed to by both parties.

Jesus Christ rebuked the Pharisees because they stood at the door without entering in and they did not allow others to enter. Some brothers turn themselves into body guards, gatemen over sisters. They serve as canopies. They monopolise the sister's time, attention, heart, yet they make no commitment.

They do not show their intention and they do not allow any other man to come near the sister. Sometimes, the sister may assume that because a brother is close to her something is going on.

Meanwhile, the brother does not understand their closeness that way. The next thing that happens is that the brother sends his wedding invitation card. This has caused problems in churches. Never get too close to a brother without knowing exactly what he has in mind. If he gets too close, pointedly ask him what he wants. He may be blocking other brothers who take it for granted that something is going on already.

Never treat men's advances like faith ministry

Many single sisters assume that once a man shows interest in them then he's the one to marry them. They then do everything to please him. The man is so cool, asks them out, take them to the family house, buys them gifts, sits them in the front seat of his car. But he does not propose marriage. Yet the sister has faith that he is the one for her. Then one day the man introduces the lady he wants to marry. Never treat a man's advance with such level of faith until he defines exactly what he wants.

Deal with attitudinal issues

Much of the attitude that some ladies put on is so bad that a man cannot even stand them. They talk anyhow, eat anyhow, behave and treat their spouse without respect. The single sister should ensure that when a man approaches her for the first time she puts on a good attitude.

The first impression lasts long. Many ladies have lost their partner due to attitudinal problem. Some have domineering spirit, they use foul language. Some easily get angry. No man would see these things and hang around.

Do not tie a partner down

Never manipulate a man into marriage. Do not use pregnancy to force a man to marry. It is not a good method and it does not last. Anything can happen along the way which might not be palatable. Many ladies end up

becoming single mothers when the men involved refuse to marry them. Avoid it.

Avoid pre-marital sex

The single sister must not let a man have carnal knowledge of her. It truncates destiny. Do not misinterpret lust for love. The man that truly loves a lady will wait. Many ladies cohabit thinking that by doing this they stand the chance of sending other ladies away. This is a lie from the pit of hell. If the man wants to abandon the lady she has been sleeping with to marry a virgin he will. Every man loves to marry a virgin, even after living a rough life.

Pray for a God-fearing partner

The fear of God is the beginning of wisdom. Prayer to have a partner who fears God is the fundamental solution to many of the challenges that people have in courtship and in marriage. The God-fearing partner will not ask for sex before marriage. He knows it is evil and there are negative spiritual consequences. The God-fearing partner will not engage in manipulation as the world does and he will treat his spouse with respect, knowing she is God's handiwork, the apple of his eyes.

Chapter Four

Nurture Tomorrow's Heroes With A Difference

aking a difference is not only about the now but the future too. Children are the future and they must be nurtured well. The seeds God has given us are tomorrow's heroes. There is a need to nurture them so that they can be the best God has destined them to be.

Nurture them with a difference. A believer should not nurture a child the way the world does. Otherwise the child will eventually follow the world, and by then all is lost. Nurturing starts from the day the baby is conceived. In order to nurture with a difference a believer must know how to give a child back to God. It is important.

When God gives a child to a family, there is a need for that child to be dedicated to God, the giver of all things. Hanna the mother of Samuel knew about this secret of giving seed back to God. She was able to key into it as recorded *1 Sam 1:27.*

1Sam.1.27 - For this child I prayed; and the LORD hath given me my petition which I asked of him:

Joseph and Mary gave Jesus back to God in *Luke 2:22.*

Luke.2.22 - And when the days of her purification according to the law of Moses were accomplished, they brought him to Jerusalem, to present him to the Lord;

This is an area so many mothers have neglected. It can be at the root of some of the challenges in marriage, and in the behavior of their children. When a mother gives her child back to God it is a confirmation of her love for God. It is a clarification of ownership; parents are caretakers, God owns children and he will watch over them.

Many make terrible mistakes by committing their seed into the hand of the state, governor, and daycare centres. From God's perspective, it's not the duty of nannies, uncles, aunties to raise the child. People engage in baby dedication in church. It is good. But nurturing the hero is not just about the ceremony aspect. There is also the spiritual aspect of it.

Raising those children spiritually means involving God in the matter. For it is not by power nor by might. The job is done by the spirit of God. As a mother, the job is not yet complete until the children raise their own children. It means what has been deposited in them is being transferred to the third generation. That is the successful mother.

A mother must ask God for grace, wisdom, knowledge and understanding to train her children. It takes the grace of God to influence a teenage child positively. The mother needs to watch her own life. It takes two to tangle. The mother that is a good role model is more likely to impact her seeds. The mother is the Bible that children read.

By the age of three a child is wise enough to know the difference between right and wrong. Teach them what is right and what is wrong. Show them love. Pray for them. Teach them to stay married, live a righteous life and put away worldliness in their character, action, behaviour. God has good plans for the child that the mother surrenders to him though payers and Godly upbringing.

Serve God with a difference

Serving God is a ministry. But the ministry referred to here is being with Jesus. To have a solid one-on-one relationship with him. This the main work, God's expectation. Every other work or responsibility in the vineyard is secondary. To be a deliverance minister is secondary. Healing the sick, raising the dead, cleaning the church, teaching in Sunday School Class, coordinating programme, taking offering on the altar, singing in the choir are all secondary The primary duty of a believer is to be with Jesus.

There are certain things that we do that might not excite God because he has his own expectations. Never mistake service for dedication to God. Never substitute work for God for the God of the work.

Do not let your personal relationship with God suffer while you are busy doing the work of God. Note that the thief on the cross did not do a single work for God. He simply ensured he had a good relationship with Christ and he made heaven. Have sound fellowship with God, one on one. Serve god at your personal altar.

One of the reasons God made man and woman was to fellowship with them. If that fellowship is broken one cannot have access to God. God rates everyone on her faithfulness more than her fruitfulness. When Jesus called the twelve disciples he wanted them to have personal fellowship with him. It is recorded thus in ***Mark 3:13-14;***

Mark. 3. 13 - And he goeth up into a mountain, and calleth unto him whom he would: and they came unto him.
Mark. 3. 14 - And he ordained twelve, that they should be with him, and that he might send them forth to preach,

God called those he wanted, and he also appointed twelve to

be with him. He had his reasons. The Bible says in Verse *14 of Mark 3* that he called them so that

> *"that they might be with him and*
> *that he might send them out..."*

The first thing is that they might be with him, and secondly that he might send them out. What matters more to God is being with him. This is where the difference is between the real woman and the fake woman. No one can be with God and her life will remain the same.

The person that is in church but is not with God will do things the same way. She is neither hot nor cold in her spiritual life. Her approach to life's issues remain the same. She does not change in her prayer life. She does not work on her attitude, behaviour etc.

How can such a person make a difference? The woman that is ready to be with God must show herself to be available, faithful, selfless and be sacrificial. She must be ready because God will place the kind of demand that a fake woman can neither understand not accept. But for the real woman, she readily gives in to God's demands. She is ready to forget the self, forget the world, and be with God. It is where the difference is between her and others, and it is how she can make a difference.

The woman with God must be different from the crowd because God does things in her and through her that the crowd cannot have access to. We have evidence in Isaiah 6:5; God is searching for vessels to be used. Isaiah saw himself as an unclean vessel.

There are vessels that are purged, vessels filled with the spirit of God as the life of Isaiah shows when he has an encounter. When

God reveals himself he does in such a way that the vessel becomes even better to be used to affect her generation. That is what being with God, ministering to God, serving God does.

How many of us are willing to be with God? How many of us can sacrifice our time, energy, just to tarry at the feet of Jesus? Enough of sitting on the fence. It is time to serve God and thereby make a difference.

Many in church are no longer offering service to God but to the self. Many have left the sight of God and are pursuing other things in church. They are busy eyeing posts, gossiping, finding fault with others, looking for the downfall of other people, trying to scatter fellowship of brethrens. They do this at the detriment of spending quality time to minister to God in the place of personal prayer. This cannot be found in the life of a real woman.

Note that it was in the place of personal service that God visited Zacharia according to *Luke 1:5;*

Luke. 1.5 - There was in the days of Herod, the king of Judaea, a certain priest named Zacharias, of the course of Abia: and his wife was of the daughters of Aaron, and her name was Elisabeth.

In the Bible, some of God's most memorable visitations happened in the place of service to him. Zacharias was at his own duty post and it was there God met him. Great things happen in the place of personal contact with God.

But many believers miss it because they focus on other issues that are not of God. Serve God, minister to him with a difference and he will make you different.

CELEBRATE GOD WITH A DIFFERENCE

Celebrating God is a total thing. It is not about the dancing in church. It is not about the singing and the special Sundays when we are asked to celebrate God. The life of a real woman celebrates God all the time. It does in her attitude, in her prayer life, in her giving, how she relates with others in church and out of church.

God must be seen in her life. She is God-conscious, celebrating him with her calm words, meekness, wisdom, always being a good example to the young and the old. She lets her life celebrate God.

No doubt, God in turn will celebrate such a woman. God will set her apart, make her shine for others to see and thereby glorify him. This is the ultimate means of making a difference.

When a believer's life celebrates God, he can go to any extent for her. This is the best way to have God set his daughter apart, make her the example he desires. For this thing is never about personal effort, it is about God who chooses who he raises, or who he brings down. May God count you worthy of his elevation in order to impact your generation in Jesus name. Amen.